雙雙中文教材 (16)
Chinese Language and Culture Course

中國詩歌欣賞 Appreciation of Chinese Poetry

王雙雙　編著

北京大学出版社
PEKING UNIVERSITY PRESS

圖書在版編目（CIP）數據

中國詩歌欣賞：繁體版／（美）王雙雙編著.—北京：北京大學出版社，2009.1
（雙雙中文教材16）
ISBN 978-7-301-14413-8

I.中… Ⅱ.王… Ⅲ.① 漢語－對外漢語教學－教材　②詩歌-文學欣賞-中國　Ⅳ.H195.4

中國版本圖書館CIP數據核字（2008）第168381號

書　　　　名：	中國詩歌欣賞
著作責任者：	王雙雙 編著
英 文 翻 譯：	王約西
插　　　圖：	王金泰
責 任 編 輯：	孫　嫻
標 準 書 號：	ISBN 978-7-301-14413-8/H・2098
出 版 發 行：	北京大學出版社
地　　　址：	北京市海淀區成府路205號　100871
網　　　址：	http://www.pup.cn
電　　　話：	郵購部 62752015　發行部 62750672　編輯部 62752028　出版部 62754962
電 子 信 箱：	zpup@pup.pku.edu.cn
印 刷 者：	北京大學印刷廠
經 銷 者：	新華書店
	889毫米×1194毫米　16開本　9.25印張　165千字
	2009年1月第1版　2009年1月第1次印刷
定　　　價：	90.00元（含課本、練習冊和CD-ROM一張）

未經許可，不得以任何方式複製或抄襲本書之部分或全部內容。
版權所有，侵權必究
舉報電話：010-62752024
電子信箱：fd@pup.pku.edu.cn

前 言

《雙雙中文教材》是一套專門爲海外青少年編寫的中文課本，是我在美國八年的中文教學實踐基礎上編寫成的。在介紹這套教材之前，請讀一首小詩：

> 一双神奇的手，
> 推开一扇窗。
> 一条神奇的路，
> 通向灿烂的中华文化。
>
> 鮑凱文　鮑維江
> 1998年

鮑維江和鮑凱文姐弟倆是美國生美國長的孩子，也是我的學生。1998年冬，他們送給我的新年賀卡上的小詩，深深地打動了我的心。我把這首詩看成我文化教學的回聲。我要傳達給海外每位中文老師：我教給他們（學生）中國文化，他們思考了、接受了、回應了。這條路走通了！

語言是交際的工具，更是一種文化和一種生活方式，所以學習中文也就離不開中華文化的學習。漢字是一種古老的象形文字，她從遠古走來，帶有大量的文化信息，但學起來並不容易。使學生增強興趣、減小難度，走出苦學漢字的怪圈，走進領悟中華文化的花園，是我編寫這套教材的初衷。

學生不論大小，天生都有求知的慾望，都有欣賞文化美的追求。中華文化本身是魅力十足的。把這宏大而玄妙的文化，深入淺出地，有聲有色地介紹出來，讓這迷人的文化如涓涓細流，一點一滴地滲入學生們的心田，使學生們逐步體味中國文化，是我編寫這套教材的目的。

為此我將漢字的學習放入文化介紹的流程之中同步進行，讓同學們在學中國地理的同時，學習漢字；在學中國歷史的同時，學習漢字；在學中國哲學的同時，學習漢字；在學中國科普文選的同時，學習漢字……

這樣的一種中文學習，知識性強，趣味性強；老師易教，學生易學。當學生們合上書本時，他們的眼前是中國的大好河山，是中國五千年的歷史和妙不可言的哲學思維，是奔騰的現代中國……

總之，他們瞭解了中華文化，就會探索這片土地，熱愛這片土地，就會與中國結下情緣。

最後我要衷心地感謝所有熱情支持和幫助我編寫教材的老師、家長、學生、朋友和家人，特別是老同學唐玲教授、何茜老師、我姐姐王欣欣編審及我女兒Uta Guo年復一年的鼎力相助。可以說這套教材是大家努力的結果。

王雙雙

說 明

　　《雙雙中文教材》是一套專門為海外學生編寫的中文教材。它是由美國加州王雙雙老師和中國專家學者共同努力，在海外多年的實踐中編寫出來的。全書共20冊，識字量2500個，包括了從識字、拼音、句型、短文的學習，到初步的較系統的中國文化的學習。教材大體介紹了中國地理、歷史、哲學等方面的豐富內容，突出了中國文化的魅力。課本知識面廣，趣味性強，深入淺出，易教易學。

　　這套教材體系完整、構架靈活、使用面廣。學生可以從零起點開始，一直學完全部課程20冊；也可以將後11冊（10～20冊）的九個文化專題和第五冊（漢語拼音）單獨使用，這樣便於開設中國哲學、地理、歷史等專門課程以及假期班、短期中國文化班、拼音速成班的高中和大學使用，符合了美國AP中文課程的目標和基本要求。

　　本書是《雙雙中文教材》的第十六冊，適用於已學習掌握約1200個漢字的學生使用。本書選取了最具代表性的古代詩詞和部分當代詩歌,所選皆為名作,各具風格。這些詩詞有描述民間生活的艱辛困苦，有抒發英雄的悲壯豪情，有對戀人的深情表白，也有對大好江山的讚歎。集中介紹詩詞的目的是讓學生欣賞中國詩詞特有的韻律美，體會中國詩詞，特別是中國古典詩詞表達情感時的豐富表現力，同時，學生們也能形象地瞭解中國古代社會生活的點滴。

編者

課程設置

年級			
一年級	中文課本（第一冊）	中文課本（第二冊）	中文課本（第三冊）
二年級	中文課本（第四冊）	中文課本（第五冊）	中文課本（第六冊）
三年級	中文課本（第七冊）	中文課本（第八冊）	中文課本（第九冊）
四年級	中國成語故事	中國地理常識	
五年級	中國古代故事	中國神話傳說	
六年級	中國古代科學技術	中國文學欣賞	
七年級	中國詩歌欣賞	中文科普閱讀	
八年級	中國古代哲學	中國歷史（上）	
九年級	中國歷史（下）	小説閱讀，中文SAT II	
十年級	中文SAT II（強化班）	小説閱讀，中文SAT II 考試	

目　錄

第一課　《詩經》與楚辭……………………………………… 1

第二課　樂府…………………………………………………… 10

第三課　唐詩（一）…………………………………………… 24

第四課　唐詩（二）…………………………………………… 33

第五課　唐詩（三）…………………………………………… 40

第六課　宋詞（一）…………………………………………… 46

第七課　宋詞（二）…………………………………………… 53

第八課　宋詞（三）…………………………………………… 62

第九課　古詩詞二首…………………………………………… 68

第十課　現代詩二首…………………………………………… 75

生字表…………………………………………………………… 85

生詞表…………………………………………………………… 89

第一課

《詩經》與楚辭

詩　經

　　《詩經》是中國第一部詩歌總集，相傳由孔子和他的學生所編，最後編定成書大約在公元前6世紀。《詩經》原名《詩》，或稱《詩三百》，共收集詩歌305篇，包括從西周初至春秋中葉五百多年間流傳的社會各個階層人士的作品。作品內容十分廣泛，反映了當時社會生活的方方面面。

　　《詩經》是中國古代詩歌的起點，對中國後世的詩歌影響深遠。

採　葛

彼採葛兮，一日不見，如三月兮！

彼採蕭兮，一日不見，如三秋兮！

彼採艾兮，一日不見，如三歲兮！

【注釋】

葛：植物名，花紫紅色，根可作藥用。

彼：那、那個；對方、他（她）。

兮：助詞，跟現代文的"啊"相似。

蕭：植物名，即青蒿(hāo)，有香氣。

艾：植物名，葉子有香氣，可用作藥材。

【詩文講解】

這是《詩經》中一首愛情詩歌。詩中描寫了情人分離的思念和痛苦：

那個姑娘採葛去了，我一天沒有見到她，就像隔了三個月呀！

那個姑娘採蕭去了，我一天沒有見到她，就像隔了三個季度那樣長啊！

那個姑娘採艾去了，我一天沒有見到她，就像隔了三年那樣長又長呀！

這首詩短短幾句，就把想念情人越來越強烈的心情生動地表現出來了。至今人們仍然用"一日不見，如隔三秋"來形容強烈的思念之情。

屈原與楚辭

屈原（約前340—前278）是戰國時期楚國人，中國歷史上第一位偉大的詩人。他創造了一種新的詩歌形式——楚辭。楚辭與《詩經》共同構成了中國詩歌的源頭。

楚辭是在南方浪漫民風的影響下，在民歌的基礎上發展起來的，詩句由自由的長短句構成。句中、句尾常用"兮"字表示語氣。這樣的詩體新鮮、生動，富有表現力。

屈原一生寫出了許多優秀的詩歌，其中最著名的是《離騷》。

《離騷》是中國古代最長的一首抒情詩。在《離騷》中，作者寫出了自己不幸的一生和被放逐後的悲憤心情，以及對楚國人民的熱愛之情。如：

長太息以掩涕兮，（我長嘆一聲禁不住流下眼淚啊，）

哀民生之多艱！（可憐人民的生活這樣多災多難！）

……

路漫漫其修遠兮，（我要走的路是多麼漫長啊，）

吾將上下而求索。（我將上天入地去追求我的理想。）

《離騷》不但感情奔放，想象浪漫神奇，而且語句美麗動人。楚辭的產生與屈原一生的遭遇和他高潔的品格是分不開的。

屈原出生在楚國一個貴族家庭。那時楚國在長江、漢水流域，是一個有五千里山河的大國。屈原早年受楚懷王信任和重用，做過高官。他主張聯合其他國家共同抵抗強大的秦國。沒想到楚懷王不但沒有採用他的主張，反而把他放逐了。屈原在被放逐的生活中時刻關心著楚國的命運。看到他熱愛的楚國一天天衰落，一次次被秦軍打敗，他悲痛萬分，寫出了《離騷》、《九歌》、《天問》等詩歌來表達內心的痛苦。最後，屈原眼見著秦軍佔領了楚國的都城，楚國滅亡了。他悲痛到極點，在農曆五月初五投汨羅江自殺。

相傳，老百姓們聽說他投江以後，馬上划船去救他，可是沒有打撈到屈原。為了不讓他的屍體被魚吃掉，人們往江裏撒米餵魚。從此以後，人們為了紀念屈原，每年農曆五月初五都要賽龍船、吃粽子，過端午節。

生詞

shōu jí 收集	collect	bēi fèn 悲憤	grief and indignation
piān 篇	chapter	yǎn 掩	cover
guǎng fàn 廣泛	wide-ranging	tì 涕	tears
fǎn yìng 反映	reflect	jīn bu zhù 禁不住	can not restrain; can't help (doing sth)
yǐng xiǎng 影響	affect; influence	qiú suǒ 求索	seek; explore
bǐ 彼	that; she; he	zhuī qiú 追求	chase
ài 艾	mugwort	lǐ xiǎng 理想	ideal
xíng shì 形式	form	zāo yù 遭遇	suffering
làng màn 浪漫	romantic	guì zú 貴族	noble; aristocrat
jī chǔ 基礎	basis; foundation	mìng yùn 命運	fate; destiny
lí sāo 離騷	*The Sorrow of Departure* (Lisao)	shuāi luò 衰落	decline
shū qíng 抒情	express one's emotion	jì niàn 紀念	commemorate
fàng zhú 放逐	banish; exile	zòng zi 粽子	*a food made of glutinous rice wrapped in bamboo leaves*

聽寫

廣泛　形式　基礎　反映　遭遇　放逐　悲憤　掩

求索　浪漫　紀念　*粽子　抒情

注：標有*號的字詞為選做題，後同。

比一比

構 { 構成 / 結構 }　　遇 { 遭遇 / 遇到 }　　仍 { 仍然 / 仍舊 }

基 { 基礎 / 基本 }　　漫 { 浪漫 / 漫長 }　　形 { 形式 / 形狀 }

詞語運用

構成　結構

楚辭與《詩經》共同構成了中國詩歌的源頭。

趙州橋是拱形結構的。

浪漫　漫長

《牛郎織女》是一個浪漫的民間故事。

中國北方的冬季十分漫長。

回答問題

1. 中國歷史上第一部詩歌總集叫什麼？

2. 《詩經》編定成書大約是在什麼時候？

3. 中國詩歌的源頭是哪兩部作品？

4. 《詩經》共有詩歌多少篇？

5. 中國歷史上第一位偉大的詩人是誰？

6. 屈原是戰國時期哪國人？

7. 請說一說中國的端午節是怎麼來的。

詞語解釋

中葉——一個歷史時期的中段。

熱愛——強烈地愛，非常愛。

構成——形成；造成；結構。

民歌——民間口頭流傳的歌曲。

紀念——對人或事表示懷念。

作品——文學藝術方面加工好的成品，如：出版的書籍、上演的影片。

 English Translation

Lesson One

Shijing and Chuci

Shijing

Shijing (The Book of Odes) is the earliest collection of Chinese poems. It's said to be compiled by Confucias and his studeats.Completed in the form of a book in approximately the sixth century B.C., it was originally called *Shi* (Poems) or *Shisanbai* (Three Hundred Poems). Covering more than five hundred years from the early Zhou Dynasty to the middle of the Spring and Autumn Period, *Shijing* includes 305 popular poems and verses written by people of all social levels. With its wide-ranging contents, *Shijing* reflects all perspectives of the social life of that time.

Shijing is the starting point of Chinese ancient poems and verses and has exerted a deep and powerful influence on the Chinese poetry of later ages.

Collecting Kudsu

My lass is away collecting kudsu,
I haven't seen her for one day only,
But it seems as long as three months truly!

My lass is away collecting mugwort,
I haven't seen her for one day only,
But it seems as long as three seasons truly!

My lass is away collecting wormwood,
I haven't seen her for one day only,
But it seems as long as three years truly!

Qu Yuan and Chuci

Qu Yuan (app. 340 – 278 B.C.) is the first great poet in the history of China. A poet of the Chu State, he created a new form of poem – chuci (a type of classical Chinese literature and a form of classical poetry typical for its local Character of the Chu State). Chuci and *Shijing* co-constitute the origin of Chinese poetry and verse.

Affected by the romantic folk customs of south China, chuci developed on the base of folk songs which consist mostly of long and short lines. In or at the end of the lines there often appears the character 兮 that makes a tone. This style of poems is fresh, vivid and expressive.

In his life, Qu Yuan wrote many excellent poems and verses. *Lisao* (the Sorrow of Departure) is one of the most well known.

In *Lisao*, the longest lyric poem in ancient China, the poet depicts his unfortunate life, his grief and indignation, and his ardent love for the Chu people. For example:

With a deep and long sigh of woe
I can't stop my tears from falling;
It's for people's misery and sorrow
That I often go bitterly weeping.

……

The road ahead for me is so long,
Step by step I walk dragging along.
To seek for ideal I'd adventure
May it be happiness or torture.

Lisao is not only overflowing with enthusiasm and full of romantic and profound feelings, but with lovely and touching lines.

The birth of chuci is closely connected with Qu Yuan's misfortune in his life and his lofty character.

Qu Yuan was born in a noble family in the Chu State which was then a large country of five thousand leagues located along the Yangtze River and the Han River. Trusted by the King of Chu (named King Huai), he was once a very high official. Nevertheless, his suggestion that the Chu State unite other countries to oppose the Qin State was unexpectedly rejected by King Huai. What is more, he was banished. During his banishment, he never stopped worrying about the fate of Chu. When he saw his beloved country deteriorating day after day and the Chu army was defeated by the Qin's, he was painfully sad and produced *Lisao*, *Jiuge* (The Nine Songs) and *Tianwen* (Heavenly Questions) etc. by which he conveyed his deep sorrow and bitterness. Finally, the capital of Chu was besieged and occupied by the Qin army. Chu perished. The fall of his motherland brought him to his extreme grief and on the fifth day of the fifth lunar month, he killed himself in the Miluo River.

On hearing his death, people rushed to his rescue on boats but in vain. To protect his body from being eaten by fish, they fed the fish by throwing rice into the river. Ever since then, on that day, it has become a traditional festival – *Duanwujie* (the Dragon Boat Festival) to memorize Qu Yuan by eating zongzi and having dragon-boat races.

第二課
樂　府

樂府開始於漢代，是國家專管音樂的一個機構，負責從民間收集詩歌。收集到的詩歌叫"樂府民歌"。這些詩歌語言樸素、生動，內容十分廣泛。其中最有名的是東漢末年的《孔雀東南飛》和南北朝時期的《木蘭辭》等。後來，詩人們把"樂府"作為一種詩體，創作了很多樂府詩。

孔雀東南飛

《孔雀東南飛》是漢樂府民歌中最優秀的敘事長詩，作者不詳。全詩340多句，說的是一對善良的青年焦仲卿(zhòngqīng)與劉蘭芝之間純真的愛情悲劇故事。千百年來，這首詩歌一直在民間流傳，深深地

打動著人們的心。

詩歌開頭為：

孔雀東南飛

五里一徘徊

一隻孤獨的孔雀在天空飛來飛去，尋找他失去的伴侶，久久不肯離去。人世間也有同樣的故事。劉蘭芝是一個美麗、勤勞、知書達禮的姑娘，詩中說她：

十三能織素

十四學裁衣

十五彈箜篌（kōng hóu）

十六誦詩書

十七歲的劉蘭芝美若天仙，嫁給了小府吏焦仲卿，夫妻倆相親相愛。可是焦仲卿為了工作經常外出，兩人相見的日子不多。蘭芝在家中天不亮就織布，三天織五匹布，婆婆還是不滿意，常常為難她。詩中寫道：

十七為君婦

心中常苦悲

君既為府吏

守節情不移

賤妾（jiàn qiè）留空房

相見常日稀

雞鳴入機織

夜夜不得息

三日斷五匹

大人故嫌遲

她實在受不了婆婆的逼迫，於是提出："既然婆婆看不上我，就請把我送回娘家吧。"焦仲卿跪在地上向母親求情：蘭芝沒有過錯，為什麼要讓她走？要是母親不肯留她，非讓她走，我一生不會再娶別人為妻了。不想母親聽了以後大怒，喝道："你竟敢不聽我的！你怎麼能替劉蘭芝說話？"

焦仲卿沒有辦法，只好含淚送蘭芝回家。分手時焦仲卿立下誓言，表示雖然蘭芝暫時回了家，但是他以後一定會再來接蘭芝。蘭芝也向天發誓，一定等著焦仲卿。

不料蘭芝回到娘家後沒有多久，縣令[①]聽說蘭芝美麗、善良，就來為兒子求婚。母親問蘭芝答應不答應，她含淚答道：

蘭芝初還時

府吏見叮嚀

結誓不別離

[①] 縣令——縣官。

母親知道蘭芝還等著焦仲卿，就讓求婚的人走了。可是過了不久，太守①又來為兒子求婚。蘭芝還是不動心。這次她哥哥不耐煩了，認為嫁給太守的兒子有錢、有地位，多麼榮耀，為什麼要等焦仲卿！在哥哥的逼迫下，蘭芝只好答應了太守家的求婚。

焦仲卿聽說後，心急如火，騎馬來見蘭芝。兩人相見，淚如雨下，感到天地之大，卻沒有他們的立足之處。於是約定，既然今生不能做夫妻，就不如一死，黃泉②下相見！

分手後，太守家迎親的隊伍來了，熱熱鬧鬧的。蘭芝在新婚之夜，痛不欲生，投水自盡。焦仲卿知道後，也上吊自殺了。詩中寫道：

我命絕今日

魂去屍長留

攬(lǎn)裙脫絲履(lǚ)

舉身赴清池

府吏聞此事

心知長別離

徘徊庭樹下

自掛東南枝

---

① 太守：漢朝管理一個郡(jùn)的最高地方官。

② 黃泉：地下的泉水，指人死後埋葬的地方。

兩家求合葬

合葬華山傍

東西植松柏

左右種梧桐（wú tóng）

枝枝相覆蓋

葉葉相交通

中有雙飛鳥

自名為鴛鴦（yuān yāng）

仰頭相向鳴

夜夜達五更（gēng）

劉蘭芝和焦仲卿死後，焦、劉兩家把他們埋葬在一起，墓邊種上了松柏和梧桐。這些樹長成了一片濃陰覆蓋的樹林，而焦仲卿和劉蘭芝死後化作林中雙飛的鴛鴦，相親相愛永不分開。

【注釋】

箜篌：一種古代樂器。

君：對人的尊稱。

賤妾：古代妻子對自己的稱呼。

絕：（呼吸）停止，死亡。

攬：用手提或抱。

履：鞋。

鴛鴦：一種鳥，雌雄成對生活在水邊。文學上常用來比喻夫妻。

五更：中國古代把一夜分為五更，到五更就到了清晨。

遊子吟

〔唐〕孟郊

慈母手中線，遊子身上衣。

臨行密密縫，意恐遲遲歸。

誰言寸草心，報得三春暉。

【注釋】

　　臨行：臨走前。

　　意：心願；心意。

　　遲：慢；晚。

　　暉：陽光。

【詩文講解】

　　這是一首樂府詩。詩中描寫慈愛的媽媽手裏拿著針線，為要遠行的兒子縫衣服。細針密線地縫呀，縫呀，生怕兒子一去幾年，遲遲不歸。難道說小草的心真的能報答春天的太陽帶給它的光和熱嗎？兒女們怎能報答母親的深情厚愛！

　　這首詩親切而真誠地歌頌了偉大的母愛，喚起天下兒女們對母親的感(ēn)恩之情。千百年來，它深深地感動著每一位讀者。

作者簡介

　　孟郊（751—814），唐代詩人。這首詩是他當了官後，回家去接母親時所作。

生詞

xù shì 敘事	narrate	bī pò 逼迫	demand forcefully; compel
jiāo 焦	Jiao (surname)	dīng níng 叮嚀	urge repeatly
liú lán zhī 劉蘭芝	Liu Lanzhi (name)	shàng diào 上吊	hang oneslf
chún zhēn 純真	pure; sincere	hún 魂	soul
bēi jù 悲劇	tragedy	sōng bǎi 松柏	pine and cypress tree
pái huái 徘徊	linger about; pace up and down	fù gài 覆蓋	cover; overlap
bàn lǚ 伴侶	companion; partner	mái zàng 埋葬	bury
qín láo 勤勞	industrious; diligent	yín 吟	chant; sing
lǎng sòng （朗）誦	read aloud with expression; recite	mèng jiāo 孟郊	Meng Jiao (name)
jià 嫁	(of a woman) marry	cí mǔ 慈母	loving and tender mother
fǔ lì 府吏	official; clerk	féng 縫	sew; stitch
wéi nán 為難	make things difficult for	huī 暉	sunshine; sunlight
xián 嫌	pick on		

聽寫

敘　純真　嫁　逼迫　朗誦　叮嚀　勤勞　嫌　慈母

郊　松柏　芝　*徘徊　伴侶

17

中國詩歌欣賞

默寫

《遊子吟》

比一比

誦（朗誦）／通（通過）

朗（朗誦）／郎（女郎）

覆（覆蓋）／復（重復）

嫌（嫌棄）／歉（道歉）

吏（官吏）／史（歷史）

徘（徘徊）／排（排隊）

柏（柏樹）／泊（湖泊）

叮｛叮嚀／叮咬｝

縫｛縫衣服／石頭縫｝

詞語運用

朗誦

班裏要開詩歌朗誦會。

老師讓我們大聲朗誦這篇課文。

爺爺朗誦詩歌特別有感情。

嫌

大家都嫌他做事太馬虎。

哥哥姐姐都嫌妹妹太嬌氣。

他總嫌自己長得矮小。

覆蓋

白雪覆蓋著大地。

幾萬年前黃土高原曾被樹木和綠草覆蓋著。

喜馬拉雅山脈終年白雪覆蓋。

為難

劉蘭芝很勤勞，每天幹很多活，可婆婆還是經常為難她。

你明明知道小妹妹怕狗，還帶狗來，這不是為難她嗎？

不耐煩

學習的時候一定要有耐心，絕對不能不耐煩。

多音字

切 (qiè)　　　　切 (qiē)

親切 (qiè)　　　刀切 (qiē)

回答問題

1. 樂府開始於哪個朝代?

2. 請說出兩首最著名的樂府詩歌。

詞語解釋

心急如火——心裏急得像火燒一樣,形容非常著急。

淚如雨下——眼淚像下雨一樣地流。

痛不欲生——悲痛得不想活下去,形容悲傷到極點。

婆婆——丈夫的媽媽。

 English Translation

Lesson Two

Yuefu

Yuefu came into being in the Han Dynasty. The name "yuefu" is the name of the official conservatory to minister songs and dances. It collected from the grassroots folksongs that were called Yuefu Folksongs. The songs embrace a rich content of social life, and the language is plain and vivid. Among these songs, the most popular ones are *Southeast the Lonesome Peacock Flies* of the late Eastern Han Dynasty and *The Ballad of Mulan* of the Northern and Southern Dynasties. Afterwards, some poets followed the style of yuefu and produced many yuefu poems.

Southeast the Lonesome Peacock Flies

Southeast the Lonesome Peacock Flies is the most excellent long narrative poem of the folksongs of Hanyuefu (Yuefu of the Han Dynasty). The poet is unknown. The poem, with its 340 and more lines, tells the tragic love story of the youths of Jiao Zhongqing and Liu Lanzhi. In the past hundreds of years, it has been circulated among the people and deeply moved the readers.

The poem starts with:

Southeast the lonesome peacock flies,
From time to time she hesitates and wanders.

A lonely peacock is flying in the sky, looking for its sweetheart here and there, not willing to fly away. The same story happens in human world. Liu Lanzhi is a pretty girl who is industrious, educated and reasonable. In the poem she says:

At the age of thirteen, I learned to weave white silk.
At fourteen I knew how to make clothes.
At fifteen I could play the Konghou.
At sixteen I could recite classical works.

Liu Lanzhi, seventeen years old, beautiful as an angel, is married to Jiao Zhongqing, a low ranking official. The two love each other dearly. Yet they can rarely meet because Jiao Zhongqing is always off on business. Alone at home, Lanzhi begins weaving before dawn, producing scores feet of cloth in three days. But her mother-in-law is not satisfied with her and often deliberately blames her for nothing. The poem says:

Since I married you at seventeen,
Always feeling miserable I have been.
Now that you work for the government all day long,
My love for you remains as strong.
Day after day I stay lonely without you,
The chances for us to meet are few.
I begin working with the day's first light,
Weaving at the loom till midnight.
I can weave scores feet of cloth in three days,
Yet your mother blames me for no reasons always.

She can no longer endure the pressure from her mother-in-law and says: Now that Mother-in-law does not like me, please send me to my mother's home. Knowing this, Jiao Zhongqing, knelling, pleads with his mother saying that Lanzhi has nothing to blame, why she should be driven away. He continues: If Mother does not want to have her here and she must leave, I would definitely not marry any other girl. His mother gets furious on his words and yells to him: How dare you refuse me! How could you possibly speak for Liu Lanzhi?

Helpless and tearing, Jiao Zhongqing sends Lanzhi to her mother's home. When parting, Jiao Zhongqing says that Lanzhi's leaving is but a short one and he will surely bring her home in near future. Lanzhi, too, vows to heaven to wait for Jiao Zhongqing.

But things happen beyond their expectation. Not long after Lanzhi comes home, the county magistrate, knowing that Lanzhi is pretty and kind, asks Lanzhi to marry his son. When Mother asked if she agrees or not, Lanzhi says with tears:

When I left for home, Zhongqing again and again
Advised me devoted I should remain.
We vowed to each other
Never to endure departure.

Mother knows that Lanzhi is still waiting for Jiao Zhongqing and she sends the runner back. Not long after that, the prefect asks Lanzhi to marry his son and she again refuses. But her brother becomes impatient. To him, the prefect's son is not only wealthy, but also with high position. It is a glorious thing for Lanzhi to marry him. Why should she wait for Jiao Zhongqing? But finally Lanzhi's brother forces her to accept the court.

When Jiao Zhongqing learns the news, he is deeply worried and rushes back on horse to see Lanzhi. They both cry bitterly when they meet. To them, although the universe is as big as it is, there is not even one inch of land for them to stay on. Therefore they both promise to die and reunite under the ground since they can not be husband and wife when they are alive.

After their departure, the prefect's escorting team of several hundred strong comes and takes Lanzhi away. At the night of the newly marriage, Lanzhi woefully ends her life in a pond. Jiao Zhongqing, too, hangs himself when he gets the news. The poem goes:

My life ends today,
My soul will wander but my body will stay.
Skirt lifted, barefooted, she waded with a strong will
Into the pond the water of which was clear and still.
When Zhongqing learned the grievous information,
He was sure Lanzhi's death was their eternal separation.
Lingering about under the courtyard tree thick and tall,
He hanged himself on its southeast brand, once and for all.
With the demand of both families-a joint funeral,
The lovers' tomb now stands on Mount Huashan's side after burial.
Pines and cypresses are planted at its east and west,
And wutong trees grow at its right and left.
The boughs and branches intertwine like the lovers' arms,
With foliage embracing one another, the world is full of charms.
Among the greens reside two birds, pretty and young,
They call themselves with the name of love-Yuanyang.
The two sing to each other with heads holding high everyday,
Their songs echo in the air till morning's first ray.

After Liu Lanzhi and Jiao Zhongqing's death, the two families bury them in one tomb. They plant pines trees and wutong trees by the grave. When the trees grow into a forest, their souls turn into two birds named Yuanyang – the symbol of love. They have never departed ever since.

The Song of a Roaming Son
[Tang] Meng Jiao

With thread and needle
My loving mother labored ceaselessly,
To make the garment for his son
Ready for traveling endlessly.

Every inch of the garment is durably made
So it'll never wear off and always fit well;
She is worried deeply in her heart for
At what time I might come home nobody can tell.

With rain and sunshine little grass grow healthy and tall,
But they can in no way return the blessing to nature.
So great and selfless is mother's love to me,
How can I in whatever way repay her in the future?

第三課

唐　詩（一）

　　唐代的詩歌是中國古代詩歌的高峰。那時詩人多達兩千，所寫的詩歌近五萬首。這些詩歌內容豐富，真實、生動地反映了唐代人民的生活。唐詩的形式多種多樣，不僅有句式自由的古體詩歌，也創造了句式固定整齊的新詩體，這就是律詩和絕句。律詩全詩共八句，每句五字的，稱五言律詩；每句七字的，稱七言律詩。絕句全詩共四句，每句五字的，稱五言絕句；每句七字的，稱七言絕句。律詩和絕句對音韻和格律的要求非常嚴格，使詩歌不但看起來形式工整、優美，而且讀起來音韻也很優美、動聽。唐代最著名的詩人有李白、杜甫(fǔ)和白居易等。

登 鸛(guàn) 雀 樓
（五言絕句）

［唐］王之渙

白日依山盡，

黃河入海流。

欲窮千里目，

更上一層樓。

【注釋】

鸛雀樓：在山西省永濟縣，位於黃河邊，是唐代的名勝。

依：依傍；緊挨著。(āi)

盡：完；到頭；全部。這裏指太陽落山。

欲：想要；希望；需要；將要。

窮：用盡。

更：再。

【詩文講解】

　　詩的前兩句描寫作者從鸛雀樓遠望的壯觀景象：傍晚，太陽在起伏的群山中慢慢落下。滾滾的黃河水向遠方奔流而去。這高山大河的壯美畫面，令詩人感嘆。隨著一步步登上樓的高層，詩人的視線越來越遠，眼界越來越開闊，使他感悟到一個哲理：只有站得更高，才能看得更遠。

望廬山瀑布
（七言絕句）

［唐］李白

日照香爐生紫煙，
遙看瀑布掛前川。
飛流直下三千尺，
疑是銀河落九天。

【註釋】

廬山：中國名山，在江西省。

香爐：指廬山的香爐峰。

九天：指天，"九"字形容天高到極點。

【詩文講解】

　　作者用誇張的手法寫出了廬山瀑布的壯麗景色：清晨，陽光照著香爐峰，紫雲裊裊(niǎo)。從遠處看去，瀑布高高地掛在石壁上。瀑布從高山頂上飛流直下，就好像是九重天上的銀河落了下來。

春 望
（五言律诗）

［唐］杜甫

國破山河在，城春草木深。

感時花濺淚，恨別鳥驚心。

烽火連三月，家書抵萬金。

白頭搔更短，渾欲不勝簪(zān)。

【注釋】

國破：指京城長安被叛(pàn)軍攻破。

烽火：古代邊防報警(jǐng)的煙火；這裏指戰爭。

家書：家信。

抵：相當於。

短：少，缺。

渾：全；這裏的意思是簡直。

簪：用來別住頭髮的一種首飾。

【詩文講解】

長安城被攻破了，可是山河還在。春天來了，長安城野草叢生。與親人分隔的痛苦使詩人見花落淚，聽到鳥的叫聲也覺得驚心。戰亂已經連續三個月了，一封家信抵得上萬兩黃金哪！白髮越搔越少，簡直連簪子都插不住了。

詩人寫這首詩時，正當安史之亂①，他身陷(xiàn)叛軍佔領下的長安城。山河破碎，家人離散，滿目荒涼的景象，使詩人感嘆戰亂給國家和人民帶來的苦難，也讓他產生了對親人強烈的思念之情。

作者簡介

杜甫（712—770），唐代偉大的現實主義詩人，生活在唐朝由強盛走向衰亡的時期。他經歷了國家的戰亂，體會到了人民生活的痛苦。杜甫的詩歌真實地反映了那個動亂時代的社會生活。他一生寫了大量詩歌，現存的有一千四百多首，被稱為"詩聖"。

---

① 安史之亂——唐朝安祿(lù)山、史思明發動的叛亂。

生詞

gù dìng 固定	fixed; permanent		lóu 樓	a multistory building
yīn yùn 音韻	rhyme and tone (of Chinese characters)		yì céng 一層	one floor
gé lǜ 格律	forms (of classical poetic composition)		kāi kuò 開闊	open; wide
yán gé 嚴格	strict; rigid		lú shān 廬山	Lushan (name of a mountain)
gōng zhěng 工整	neat and orderly		pù bù 瀑布	waterfall
dòngtīng 動聽	pleasant to listen to		fēng huǒ 烽火	beacon-fire; flames of war
dēng 登	ascend; mount		sāo 搔	scratch

背誦並默寫

《登鸛雀樓》和《望廬山瀑布》（"鸛"字可以用拼音）

比一比

$$\begin{cases} 瀑（瀑布）\\ 爆（爆炸） \end{cases} \quad \begin{cases} 烽（烽火）\\ 峰（山峰） \end{cases} \quad 層\begin{cases} 一層\\ 地層 \end{cases}$$

$$\begin{cases} 樓（高樓）\\ 摟（摟著） \end{cases} \quad \begin{cases} 登（登山）\\ 瞪（瞪眼） \end{cases} \quad 律\begin{cases} 格律\\ 紀律 \end{cases}$$

回答問題

1. 中國古代詩歌的高峰是什麼時候？

2. 唐代創造了哪兩種新詩體？

3. 唐代最著名的詩人有誰？請至少說出三位詩人。

4. 選做題：“日照香爐生紫煙，遙看瀑布掛前川。飛流直下三千尺，疑是銀河落九天。”其中哪一句採用了誇張的想象？

朗讀

唐詩三首

Lesson Three
Tang Poems（Part I）

    The poems of the Tang Dynasty mark the highlights of the ancient Chinese poetry. During that period, about 2,000 poets produced almost 50,000 poems. The Tang poems, with their rich contents, reflect the life of the Tang people truly and expressively. The style of Tang poems varies a great deal, including the old style, the sentences structure of which are rather free, and newly created styles, the sentence structures of which are strictly fixed as lushi and jueju. A lushi is a poem of eight lines. If one line of which contains five characters, it is called wuyanlushi (pentasyllabic regulated verse). If one line of which contains seven characters, it is called qiyanlushi (heptusyllabic regulated verse). There are four lines in a jueju. If one line of which contains five characters, it is called wuyanjueju (pentusyllabic quatrain). If seven characters, it is a qiyanjueju (heptasyllabic quatrain). Both lushi and jueju are composed with strict tonal patterns and rhyme schemes so that they not only look neat and graceful, but also read pleasant to ears. The famous poets of the Tang Dynasty include Li Bai, Du Fu and Bai Juyi, etc.

Ascending the Stork Tower
(a wuyanjueju)

[Tang] Wang Zhihuan

Behind the mountains is the setting sun,
To the East Sea we see the Yellow River run.
If you wish to get a better view of the world,
To climb a higher story is all to be done.

The View of the Lushan Waterfall
(a qiyanjueju)

[Tang] Li Bai

Sunlight has put Xianglu Peak in purplish haze,
From far away I attentively gaze.
On a steep a water-fall hanging,
Down from a 3,000-foot height, roaring;
As if it has fallen into sight right away,
From the Ninth Heaven's Milky Way.

The Spring Prospect
(a wuyanlüshi)

[Tang] Du Fu

My country has been destroyed,
But mountains and rivers remain;
When spring arrives as expected,
Weeds and trees grow all the same.
The wilderness blooms without delay.
This brings up my tears sad,
Departed have I and my family for long,
Even the chirps of birds frighten me mad.
For three months the savage war continues,
Allowing no mails for people to receive and hold;
A letter from home coming through iron and blood,
Is so dear no one'd swap for ten thousand in gold.
My hair is turning scarce and white,
And thinner still when scratched by hand;
When I try to put a hairpin on,
Without help it can not stand.

第四課

唐 詩（二）

將(qiāng)進酒

[唐] 李白

君不見，黃河之水天上來，

奔流到海不復回。

君不見，高堂明鏡悲白髮，

朝如青絲暮成雪。

人生得意須盡歡，

莫使金樽(zūn)空對月。

天生我材必有用，

千金散盡還復來。

烹羊宰牛且為樂，

會須一飲三百杯。

岑(cén)夫子，丹丘生，

將進酒，杯莫停。

與君歌一曲,

請君為我傾耳聽。

鐘鼓饌(zhuàn)玉何足貴,

但願長醉不願醒。

古來聖賢皆寂寞,

惟有飲者留其名。

陳王昔時宴平樂(lè),

斗酒十千恣(zì)歡謔(xuè)。

主人何為言少錢，

徑須沽取對君酌。

五花馬，千金裘，

呼兒將出換美酒，

與爾同銷萬古愁。

【注釋】

將進酒：將，念作qiāng，請；將進酒，請喝酒。

樽：古代盛酒的器具，酒杯。

烹：煮。

岑夫子、丹丘生：指李白的兩個朋友。

傾耳聽：傾，歪倒；傾耳聽，用力傾聽，這裏指仔細聽。

鐘鼓：鳴鐘擊鼓作樂，這裏指富貴人家的音樂。

饌玉：饌，飲食；玉，像玉一樣美好；饌玉，珍美如玉的飲食。

聖賢：指品格高尚、才智過人的人。

陳王：即曹植。

昔時：從前。

宴平樂："平樂"為一道觀(guàn)名；曹植《名都篇》中有"歸來宴平樂，美酒斗十千"的詩句。

恣：任意。

謔：開玩笑。

沽：買。

酌：斟酒；飲酒。（zhēn）

將出：將，念作jiāng，拿。

爾：你。

銷：除去，消除。

【詩文講解】

這首詩是在李白初入京城，失意而歸，與朋友相會時寫下的一首"勸酒歌"。

難道你沒有看見黃河之水從高天奔流而下，東入大海，如時光奔流不回？難道你沒有看見鏡中的黑髮，轉眼間已變為雪白，是多麼令人傷悲！然而，人生並不是一杯苦酒，還是和朋友們痛快地飲酒談笑吧，不要讓精美的酒杯空對明月。"天生我材必有用"，千金散盡還會有的。功名富貴，不過是過眼煙雲。朝廷（tíng）讓人失望，金錢、物品都不必珍惜，只有美酒可以消愁。

這首詩雖然流露出詩人對自己得不到重用的感嘆，但還是表達了豪放、樂觀的情懷，是一部不可多得的好作品，是李白的代表作之一。

作者簡介

李白（701—762），唐代最偉大的浪漫主義詩人。他的詩歌想象力驚人，風格豪放，使人過目難忘。李白常用高度誇張的手法來表達強烈的感情。他一生寫了很多詩歌，現存的有一千多首，被稱為"詩仙"。

第四課

生詞

mò 莫	not; don't	yàn 宴	banquet
pēng 烹	cook; boil	jìng zhí 徑（直）	straight; directly
qīngtīng 傾聽	listen attentively	gū 沽	purchase
shèngxián 聖賢	sages and men of virtue	zhuó 酌	drink; pour out (wine)
jì mò 寂寞	lonesome; lonely	qiú 裘	fur coat
xī shí 昔時	in the past	chóu 愁	worry; distress

背誦並默寫

《將進酒》的前八句

比一比

宴 { 宴會 / 宴請 }　　聖 { 聖賢 / 聖人 }　　傾 { 傾倒 / 傾聽 }

根據課文選擇正確答案

1. 《將進酒》的作者是_____。

　A. 孟郊　　　　　B. 杜甫　　　　　C. 李白

37

2. "君不見黃河之水天上來,奔流到海不復回"

    比喻_____。

    A.黃河的源頭太高   B.河水不會倒流   C.時光飛快過去

3. "君不見高堂明鏡悲白髮,朝如青絲暮成雪"

    比喻_____。

    A.頭髮白得早   B.人生短暫   C.鏡子不好

4. "天生我材必有用,千金散盡還復來"

    表達了李白_____的心情。

    A.自信、樂觀   B.痛恨   C.悲傷

Lesson Four

Tang Poems (Part II)

Let's Drink More
[Tang] Li Bai

Don't you see the Yellow River roaring from the sky,
Surging to the East Sea and never coming back?
Don't you see the mirror in the hall lamenting your hair,
Now snowy white but in the morning pitch-black?
Elate, you should drink to your full without stop, alas!
Never let the moon accompany your empty wine glass.

We are born talents
And we must be useful in some way.
A thousand taels of gold may be spent,
But they can be earned again someday.
Slaughter a cow and cook a lamb,
We enjoy ourselves freely,
After three hundred glasses of wine,
Clear-minded we remain joyfully.
Cen and Qiu, my dear friends,
Fill you glass and bottom up.
I invite you to more wine,
Glass after glass let's drink, don't stop!
I will now sing a song for you,
Please listen to me, the chances are few.
Excellent food and beautiful music,
Matter not to us whatever.
All I wish is to stay drunk,
Sober will we become never.
From ancient time the masterminds
Were all well forgotten;
Only those heavy drinkers whose names
Are still in people's mind written.
Cao Zhi in his poem mentions
His feast in Ping'le a Taoist temple of that time,
Where ten thousand taels of gold
Can only buy one cask of wine.
The host needs not complain about our lack of money,
To drink with you I would surely sell everything worthy.
I would sell my dappled horse
And my dear fur coat you will rarely find,
With the money we can buy more beautiful wine,
So that all the sorrows may slip from our mind.

第五課

唐　詩（三）

賣炭翁

［唐］白居易

賣炭翁，

伐薪燒炭南山中。

滿面塵灰煙火色，

兩鬢蒼蒼十指黑。（hè）

賣炭得錢何所營？

身上衣裳口中食。

可憐身上衣正單，

心憂炭賤願天寒。

夜來城外一尺雪，

曉駕炭車輾冰轍。（zhé）

牛困人飢日已高，

市南門外泥中歇。

翩翩兩騎來是誰？（jì）

黃衣使者白衫兒。
手把文書口稱敕(chì)，
迴車叱牛牽向北。
一車炭，千餘斤，
宮使驅將惜不得！
半匹紅紗一丈綾，
繫向牛頭充炭值。

【注釋】

伐薪燒炭：砍柴，將木柴燒成炭。

兩鬢蒼蒼：耳朵前邊的頭髮都白了。

何所營：做什麼用？

衣正單：穿的衣服很單薄。

心憂炭賤：擔心木炭的價錢太低。

輾冰轍：車輪壓在路面的冰雪上，輾出車轍。

牛困人飢：牛累了，人餓了。

敕：帝王的命令，詔書。（zhào）

叱：大聲責罵。

千餘斤：一千多斤。

宮使驅將惜不得：宮裏的人拿走了，心疼也沒辦法。

充炭值：值，價值；算作買炭的錢。

作者簡介

白居易（772—846），唐代著名詩人。父親是個小官。父親去世後，家庭生活困苦，因此白居易比較瞭解社會現實生活。他一生留下的詩作將近三千首，作品通俗易懂，反映了人民生活的疾苦，表達了詩人的同情之心。相傳他寫好詩以後，都要先讀給不識字的老媽媽聽，老媽媽聽懂了，他纔拿出去，因此他的詩在社會上流傳很廣。

生詞

fá 伐	fell; chop		piān piān 翩翩	elegant; lightly
xīn 薪	firewood		chì 叱	rebuke loudly
liǎng bìn 兩鬢	the temples		qiān 牽	lead (by holding the leash)
yōu 憂	worried; sad		qū 驅	drive; expel
jiàn 賤	cheap		shā 紗	gauze
jià chē 駕車	draw a cart		líng 綾	damask silk
niǎn 輾	crush		jì 繫	fasten; tie
jī 飢	hungry		jià zhí （價）值	price; value
xiē 歇	take a rest			

背誦並默寫

《賣炭翁》前八句

比一比

- 伐（伐木）
- 代（古代）

- 飢（飢餓）
- 肌（肌個）

營
- 營養
- 經營

- 薪（薪水）
- 新（新年）

- 紗（紗布）
- 沙（沙土）

惜
- 可惜
- 愛惜

詞語運用

駕車
下雨天駕車，要特別注意安全。
駕車時最好不要打手機。

價值
這輛高級跑車價值90,000美元。
這臺手提電腦價值8,000元。

回答問題

1. 賣炭翁的工作辛苦不辛苦？
2. 他準備用賣炭的錢來做什麼？
3. 天那麼冷，賣炭翁衣服穿得暖和嗎？
4. 賣炭翁的衣服穿得很單薄，為什麼他還希望天氣寒冷呢？
5. 宮使給賣炭翁很少的東西就拿走一大車炭，公平不公平？

 English Translation

Lesson Five

Tang Poems (Part III)

The Charcoal Vender
[Tang] Bai Juyi

The old charcoal vender in Mount Nanshan,
Hews wood and makes charcoal.
Covered by dust and smoked by heat,
His face looks dark and dirty and all.
Temples grey, fingers black,
Hard life has bent his back.
Daily clothes and daily foods
Are all he's for to sell his goods.
In thin coat he cannot but shiver,
But he wants it colder, for the price may be higher.
One foot deep the night's snow has fallen,
Covering all outside the city wall olden.
With his ox cart setting off before the first glow,
Wheels leaving ruts clear in dazzling snow.
Ox tired, driver hungry, the sun has risen high,
Outside the south gate in the mud a rest they can't deny.
Dressed in yellow and white garments,
Two horse riders are coming swiftly around.
With orders from His Majesty, documents of the Court,
The Emperor's men force the cart and ox northbound.
A thousand catties and more
The cartload of charcoal must weigh.
But in face of the emperor's power and bully,
It's unfair, but submission is the only way,
They put on the ox horn half a bolt of red silk
And bits of satin on His Majesty's behalf,
As payment of the cartload of charcoal,
But it does not cover the cost, not even half.

第六課

宋 詞（一）

"詞"早在唐代就已經有了，但是到了宋代，詞才真正流行起來。詞按不同的格式填寫，句子有長有短，更有表現力。《全宋詞》一書中，收集了一千三百多人的兩萬多首詞。詞的創作到宋代達到了高峰，最有名的詞作者有蘇軾(shì)、陸游等。

念奴嬌·赤壁懷古①

［北宋］蘇軾

大江東去，

浪淘盡、

千古風流人物。

故壘西邊，

人道是、

三國周郎赤壁。

---

① 念奴嬌·赤壁懷古——念奴嬌是一個詞牌名（詞調的名稱），《赤壁懷古》是詞的題目。赤壁，地名，在今中國湖北省。

亂石穿空，

驚濤拍岸，

捲(juǎn)起千堆雪。

江山如畫，

一時多少豪傑！

遙想公瑾當年，

小喬初嫁了，

雄姿英發。

羽扇綸巾，

談笑間、

強虜①灰飛煙滅。

故國神遊，

多情應笑我，

早生華髮。

人生如夢，

一樽(zūn)還酹(lèi)江月。

---

① 在有的版本中"強虜"也作"檣櫓(qiáng lǔ)"。

【注釋】

懷古：追念古代的事情。

風流人物：這裏指英雄人物。

故壘：古代軍營的牆壁或工事。

周郎：指周瑜。

公瑾：周瑜的字。

雄姿：英武的樣子。

小喬：三國時期最有名的美人之一。

綸巾：古代配有青絲帶的頭巾。

強虜：強大的敵人。

酹：把酒灑在地上，表示紀念。

【詩文講解】

這是蘇軾遊赤壁時寫下的一首名作。

波瀾壯闊的歷史，就像滾滾東流的長江水，後浪推前浪，永不停息。千百年來，在中華大地上發生了多少驚天動地的事件，涌現出多少氣勢非凡的英雄。江岸上古跡的西邊，聽說是三國時周瑜大破曹軍的赤壁古戰場。那裏，巨石高聳，直入雲間，洶涌的江水拍打著岸邊，層層浪花像一堆堆白雪。如此美好的江山，哺育出多少英雄豪傑！

回想周瑜當年，年輕、英武。美麗的小喬嫁給了他。他與才智過人的諸葛亮在從容的談笑中，制定出了打敗曹軍的計劃，一把火燒得曹軍戰船灰飛煙滅，建立了赫赫戰功。

重遊古戰場，詩人笑自己對歷史太動情了，以致早早地白了頭髮。

緬懷古人，對照自己，詩人感傷自己年紀老大還沒有建功立業，不由感嘆道：人生短暫，真像一場夢啊！暫且舉起酒杯，將酒倒入江中，來祭月亮吧！

作者簡介

蘇軾（1037—1101）是北宋時期的大文學家、書法家、畫家，在中國文學史上佔有重要地位。在詩歌創作方面，他開創了豪放詞派，對後世有很大的影響。《念奴嬌·赤壁懷古》是千古傳誦的傑作，也是蘇軾的代表作之一。後人用這個詞調的時候，有的就用"大江東去"或"酹江月"來代替"念奴嬌"，由此可見這首詞的名氣和影響有多大！

生詞

奴 nú	slave	姿 zī	appearance
淘 táo	wash	綸巾 guān jīn	silk hood
豪傑 háo jié	hero	虜 lǔ	enemy; captive
公瑾 gōng jǐn	Gongjin (another name of Zhou Yu)		

默寫

《念奴嬌·赤壁懷古》前十一行

比一比

$$\begin{cases} 嫁（出嫁） \\ 家（家庭） \end{cases}$$

$$傑\begin{cases} 豪傑 \\ 傑出 \end{cases}$$

$$\begin{cases} 豪（富豪） \\ 毫（毫毛） \end{cases}$$

$$格\begin{cases} 格式 \\ 格子 \end{cases}$$

詞語運用

捲 (juǎn)

風捲著烏雲。

岸邊停放的小船，被海浪捲走了。

卷 (juàn)

《本草綱目》全書共52卷。

老師拿著考卷走進教室。

根據課文選擇正確答案

1. 《念奴嬌·赤壁懷古》的作者是_____。

　　A.李白　　　　　　B.杜甫　　　　　　C.蘇軾

2. 《念奴嬌·赤壁懷古》是_____。

　　A.詩　　　　　　　B.詞　　　　　　　C.楚辭

3. 蘇軾是_____的大文學家。

　　A.宋朝　　　　　　B.戰國　　　　　　C.唐朝

詞語解釋

江山——江河和山嶺,常用來指國家。

背誦

《念奴嬌·赤壁懷古》

English Translation

Lesson Six

Song Ci (Part I)

Ci (poetry in ci form or ci poetry) existed as early as in the Tang Dynasty, but it became popular in the Song Dynasty. Ci is written strictly according to specific tonal patterns. The lines can be long or short so that they can convey the poet's feelings more powerfully. *A Complete Collection of Song Ci* contains more than 20,000 ci by more than 1,300 poets. Ci reached its peak in the Song Dynasty. The most famous ci poets include Su Shi and Lu You, etc.

Thinking Back on the Red Cliff
to the tonal pattern of *Niannujiao*
[Northern Song] Su Shi

The great Yangtze surges east,
Washing away
All the heroic men in the past thousands of years.
West of the ancient fortress-they say -
Is the Red Cliff where the glorious victories of
Zhou Yu of the Three Kingdoms' time stay.
Rugged steeps scrape the sky,
Mountainous waves rip the shores,
Churning thousands of snow mounds with roars.
Among these mountains and rivers beautiful as paintings,
Countless heroes have gained their doings!

We think of Gongjin of those years -
When he just married Qiao the younger -
With plumed fan and silk hood,
Showing a heroic and vigorous posture.
He talked and laughed
While in flames and smoke o's er his foes he triumphed.
When visiting this ancient battlefield sentimentally,
So impressed and moved I see my hair turned grey untimely.
Although life is like a dream passing soon,
Still I toast to the River and the Moon!

第七課

宋　詞（二）

釵　頭　鳳①

［南宋］陸游

紅酥手，黃滕(téng)酒。

滿城春色宮牆柳。

東風惡，歡情薄，

一懷愁緒，幾年離索。

錯！錯！錯！

春如舊，人空瘦，

淚痕紅浥(yì)鮫綃(jiāo xiāo)透。

桃花落，閒池閣，

山盟雖在，錦書難託。

莫！莫！莫！

---

① 釵頭鳳——詞牌名。

中國詩歌欣賞

【注釋】

　　紅酥手：女人紅潤細嫩的手。

　　黃縢酒：古代的一種酒。

　　東風：這裏比喻詩人的母親。

　　歡情薄：美滿的愛情遭到破壞。

　　一懷愁緒：滿心的愁苦。

　　離索：別離。

　　春如舊，人空瘦：春天還是如期而至，但心上人已憔悴不堪。

　　淚痕紅浥鮫綃透：浥，沾濕；鮫綃，手帕、絲巾；淚水滴落，濕透了絲帕。

　　桃花落，閒池閣：春天將盡，桃花散落，池水邊樓閣上，再沒有人

來約會遊玩了。

山盟雖在，錦書難託：原來立下的海誓山盟還在心中，但是現在兩人相互間連信都不能寫了。

【詩文講解】

早年，陸游曾娶唐琬(wǎn)為妻，詞的開頭就追憶了唐琬的美麗和以前兩人之間幸福美滿的愛情生活。但是因為婆婆不喜歡唐琬，活活把他們分開了。幾年後的一個春天，陸游在家鄉的沈(shěn)園又碰到已嫁給別人的唐琬，心中悲傷，於是提筆在沈園的牆壁上寫下了這首詞，表達了美滿愛情被破壞以後深深的痛苦。

作者簡介

陸游（1125—1210），南宋愛國詩人。他生活的時代，正是南宋不斷受到金國入侵(qīn)的時代。陸游也做過官，堅決主張抗金。他一生留下九千多首詩，其中許多詩反映了他抗金愛國的熱情。

釵 頭 鳳

［南宋］唐琬

世情薄，人情惡，

雨送黃昏花易落。

曉風乾，淚痕殘，

欲箋心事，獨語斜闌。

難！難！難！

人成各，今非昨，

病魂常似鞦韆索。

角聲寒，夜闌珊，

怕人尋問，嚥淚裝歡。

瞞！瞞！瞞！

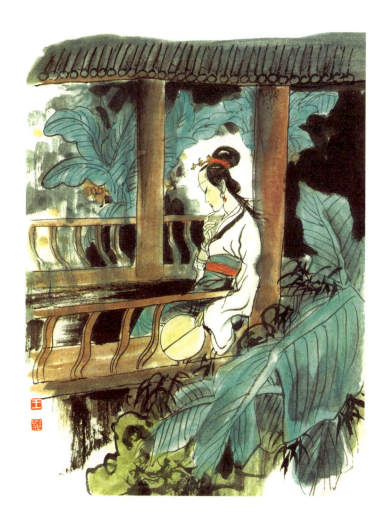

【注釋】

曉風：晨風。

淚痕殘：臉上留下眼淚的痕跡。

欲箋心事：想要寫信說說心事。

斜闌：這裏"闌"同"欄"。斜闌，斜靠著欄杆。

人成各，今非昨：現在不比以前，她與陸游已成為互不相干的兩個人了。

鞦韆索：鞦韆的繩子。

角聲寒：號角聲淒涼。qī

夜闌珊：闌珊，將盡；夜闌珊，黑夜快要過去了。

【詩文講解】

對唐琬來說，世間的人情太冷、太薄。她與陸游這對恩愛(ēn)夫妻被婆婆活活拆散。她覺得自己就像在黃昏中被風雨吹打的花，滿身是傷。一夜夜的淚水，一次次地被晨風吹乾，滿心的痛苦又能向誰訴說？只能獨自靠著欄杆嘆息："難！難！難！"

唐琬感到自己的命運就像鞦韆上的繩子，飄飄盪盪，不能自主。更不幸的是唐琬改嫁後，連表達悲苦的自由都沒有了。長夜無眠，聽著淒涼的號角聲，讓人心碎，直到天明，又"怕人尋問，嚥淚裝歡"，只能"瞞！瞞！瞞！"

據說唐琬作此詞後不久就去世了。這首詞表達了她對封建禮法的不滿和她內心的巨大痛苦。如泣如訴，真切感人。

生詞

chāi 釵	an ornament worn on the hair by women	lèi hén 淚痕	tear stains
sū 酥	soft; frail	cán 殘	remaining
qíng xù （情）緒	mood	jiān 箋	writing paper
shānméng hǎi shì 山盟（海誓）	a solemn pledge of enduring love	xié 斜	slanting; tilted
jǐn 錦	brocade	lán 闌	railing; fence
tuō 託	entrust	yàn 嚥	swallow

默寫

《釵頭鳳》（陸游）前五行（生字可以用漢語拼音）

詞語運用

情緒

比賽之前，隊員們情緒高漲，信心十足。

根據課文選擇正確答案

1. 陸游是_____的人。

   A.漢朝　　　　　　B.唐朝　　　　　　C.宋朝

2. 陸游《釵頭鳳》是一首_____。

   A.詩　　　　　　　B.詞　　　　　　　C.楚辭

3. "春如舊，人空瘦"意思是_____。

   A.春天如期而至，但心上人已憔悴不堪

   B.春天來了，人很瘦

詞語解釋

　　山盟海誓──男女相愛立下的誓言和盟約，表示愛情要像山和海那樣永遠不變。

背　誦

　　《釵頭鳳》（陸游）

 English Translation

Lesson Seven

Song Ci (Part II)

To the Tonal Pattern of *Chaitoufeng*
[Southern Song] Lu You

So soft and pink are your hands,
So savory and mellow is the wine.
Willow twigs hang o' or the palace wall,
Reporting the arrival of spring time.
Merciless mother destroyed our marriage life,
Our happiness will hence return never.
Ever since our departure many years have passed,
My sorrow and bitterness will last for ever.
All this is Wrong! Wrong! Wrong!

Spring has come again as usual,
Grievance has turned you weak and lean.
Your silk clothes are wet all through,
'ause tears run down like a stream.
Peach flower petals falling, spring leaving,
Pond and pavilion remain, but without thee.
Though our vow for love still lingers in the air,
I can't send letters to you, nor you to me.
Let it not happen again. No! No! No!

To the Tonal Pattern of *Chaitoufeng*
[Southern Song] Tang Wan

Cruel is the world,
Cold is people's heart.
Evening gusts and rain
Forcing petals to fall apart.
Morning breeze dried my eyes,
Trace of weeping almost disappears.
I'm eager to speak out my mind, but I can only
Lean on the fence talking to myself in tears.
Life is really Hard! Hard! Hard!

The two of us have separated totally,
Today has nothing to do with yesterday.
The sick body hangs on feebly,
Like the ropes of a swing-weakly sway.
Desolating is the sound of bugles,
Sleepless is the night breaking.
For fear of being asked about the truth,
I have to keep to my own mind everything.
My real world? Hide! Hide! Hide!

第八課

宋　詞（三）

滿江紅①·寫懷

〔南宋〕 岳飛

怒髮衝冠，

憑闌處、

瀟瀟雨歇。

抬望眼、

仰天長嘯，

壯懷激烈。

三十功名塵與土，

八千里路雲和月。

莫等閒、

白了少年頭，

空悲切。

---

① 滿江紅——詞牌名。

第八課

靖(jìng)康恥，

猶未雪。

臣子恨，

何時滅。

駕長車、

踏破賀蘭山缺。

壯志飢餐胡虜肉，

笑談渴飲匈奴血。

待從頭、

收拾舊山河，

朝天闕。

【注釋】

憑闌處：靠著欄杆站立。

瀟瀟：雨聲。

嘯：這裏指長聲喊叫。

壯懷激烈：壯志在心中激盪。

等閑：隨隨便便；輕易。

白了少年頭：青少年變成了白髮老人。

空悲切：一事無成而傷心悲哀。

靖康恥：指靖康元年（1126年）金軍攻下宋朝首都，第二年又擄走宋朝皇帝及貴族大臣等三千多人，北宋從此滅亡的事件。

猶未雪：（恥辱）還沒洗掉。

賀蘭山缺：賀蘭山，山名，在中國西北。缺，缺口，這裏指山口。

胡虜：外敵，這裏指金國人。

匈奴：這裏指中國北方、西北地區其他的民族，主要指金國人。

朝天闕：闕(liào)，皇宮門前兩邊的瞭望樓，這裏指皇宮；朝天闕，朝見皇帝。

【詩文講解】

瀟瀟的細雨停了，岳飛站在高處的欄杆前，放眼遠望，悲憤之情從心中湧出；抬起頭向著長空大喊一聲，誓死打敗金兵收復國土的壯志在心中激盪。他回想一生轉戰萬里抗敵報國的經歷，更感到收復失地的緊迫，不能白白地浪費時間了。他想到靖康年的國恥至今未報，作為國家的大臣，內心怎能平靜呢？他要駕著戰車直衝到賀蘭山下，與敵人決一死戰。等到打敗了敵人的那一天，再重新修建可愛的家園。

這是一首千古傑作，表達了岳飛希望報仇雪恨、收復國土的悲壯心情。

作者簡介

岳飛（1103—1142）南宋抗金名將。他主張抗金，帶領南宋軍隊多次打敗金軍，收復失去的疆土。但是皇帝和大臣秦檜(huì)一心求和，將岳飛殺害。

生詞

憑 píng	lean on		猶 yóu	stilll; even
瀟瀟 xiāoxiāo	whistling and pattering		踏 tà	step on; tread
嘯 xiào	roar; howl		匈奴 xiōng nú	Hun (an ancient nationality in China)
激烈 jī liè	violent; fierce		闕 què	watchtower on either side of a palace gate
恥 chǐ	shame			

默寫

《滿江紅·寫懷》前十一行

根據課文選擇正確答案

1. 《滿江紅・寫懷》的作者是＿＿＿＿＿。

    A.岳飛　　　　　B.李白　　　　　C.蘇軾

2. 岳飛是＿＿＿＿＿人。

    A.漢朝　　　　　B.唐朝　　　　　C.宋朝

3. 《滿江紅・寫懷》表達了岳飛＿＿＿＿＿。

    A.希望報仇雪恨、收復國土的悲壯心情

    B.收回了國土的快樂心情

詞語解釋

怒髮衝冠——頭髮直豎，把帽子都頂起來了。形容非常憤怒。

背誦

《滿江紅・寫懷》

 *English Translation*

Lesson Eight

Song Ci (Part III)

Expressing My Mind
to the tonal pattern of *Manjianghong*
[Southern Song] Yue Fei

Furious rage surging up to my helmet,
I lean on the railing.
It has stopped drizzling.
Lifting my eyes,
Towards the blue I give up to a roar,
I can not press my anger any more.
Nothing is thirty years of rank and reputations,
The moon and clouds see eight hundred leagues of expeditions.
Do not fool away your time.
Your hair turns white when you see in pain,
Grieve and regret you may but well in vain.

The national insult of Jingkang
Is still to be avenged wholly.
As to people's heartfelt hatred,
When shall it be cleared entirely?
We should ride our chariots of war,
To crush those foes in Helan Mountain's passes hiding.
Heroes! Eat the flesh of our foes when hungry.
Thirsty, drink Hun's blood chatting and laughing.
Let us begin immediately
Resuming our mountains and rivers.
When it is done, report to His Majesty.

第九課

古詩詞二首

相見歡①

［南唐］李煜(yù)

無言獨上西樓，

月如鉤。

寂寞梧桐深院鎖清秋。

剪不斷，

理還亂，

是離愁。

別是一番滋味在心頭。

【注釋】

寂寞：孤單，冷清。

離愁：離別之苦。

---

① 相見歡——詞牌名。

第九課

【詩文講解】

獨自登上西樓,靜靜地遙望茫茫夜空,一彎殘月,照著庭院裏的梧桐。這樣寂寞、冷清的秋色也被鎖在高牆深院中。然而,"鎖"住的又何止是這滿院的秋色?詩人心亂如麻:"剪不斷,理還亂,是離愁"。這種愁苦的滋味真是説不出地難受啊!

作者簡介

李煜(937—978)是南唐最後一位皇帝,也是一位傑出的詞人。他當皇帝時,南唐國力已經很弱,而宋強大起來。他一方面每年送金銀等物給宋去討(tǎo)好,另一方面又在生活上盡情享(xiǎng)樂。後來,南唐被宋所滅,他自己也成了囚(qiú)徒。這首《相見歡》就是他被囚禁之時寫的。

過零丁洋

[南宋] 文天祥(xiáng)

辛苦遭逢起一經，
干戈寥落四周星。
山河破碎風飄絮，
身世浮沉雨打萍。

惶恐灘頭說惶恐，

零丁洋裏嘆零丁。

人生自古誰無死，

留取丹心照汗青。

【注釋】

起一經：經，指四書五經；起一經，一生的艱辛就是從學習四書五經開始的。

四周星：四年光陰。

風飄絮：隨風亂飄的柳絮。

身世：指人生的經歷、遭遇。

惶恐灘：地名。

惶恐：驚慌、害怕。

零丁洋：地名。

零丁：同"伶仃"(língdīng)；孤苦伶仃，沒有依靠。

留取：留下。

丹心：紅心，對祖國、民族忠誠的心。

汗青：史册(cè)，史書。

【詩文講解】

小時苦讀經書，立下保衛國家的遠大志向。長大後做了官，正遇上元軍入侵南宋。經過四年抗元戰爭，不幸被俘(fú)。眼看著祖國的山河被敵軍破壞得像四散的柳絮，自己的一生如同風雨中飄盪的浮萍。自古以來人都

有一死，我要把這顆對祖國的忠心永遠留在史冊上。

作者在詩中回憶了自己抵抗元兵、保衛國家的艱難戰鬥，寫出了山河破碎的痛苦，最後兩句詩表現了作者視死如歸的英雄氣概。

作者簡介

文天祥（1236—1283），南宋末年政治家和愛國詩人，生於江西，二十歲中狀（zhòng）元。當元兵大舉進攻南宋時，他組織軍隊抵抗，後來兵敗被俘，1283年被殺害。囚禁中，文天祥寫下了《過零丁洋》一詩。詩中"人生自古誰無死，留取丹心照汗青"一句成為千古絕句，傳誦至今。

生詞

gōu 鈎	hook; crescent		zī wèi 滋味	taste; feeling
wú tóng 梧桐	Chinese parasol tree		líng 零	zero
suǒ 鎖	lock up; lock		gān gē 干戈	arms; weapons of war
jiǎn 剪	cut; trim		liáo luò 寥落	scattered; sparse
fān 番	a kind of		fú píng （浮）萍	duckweed

背誦並默寫

李煜的《相見歡》

文天祥的詩句"人生自古誰無死，留取丹心照汗青"

比一比

逢 { 相逢 / 重逢 }　　寥 { 寥落 / 寥寥無幾 }　　浮 { 浮動 / 浮雲 / 浮萍 }

恐 { 惶恐 / 恐怕 }　　寂 { 寂寞 / 寂靜 }　　{ 番（一番）/ 翻（翻開）}

根據課文選擇正確答案

1. 《相見歡》（無言獨上西樓）的作者是＿＿＿＿＿。

　　A.李白　　　　B.李煜

2. 李煜是南唐的＿＿＿＿＿。

　　A.皇帝　　　　B.將軍

3. "人生自古誰無死，留取丹心照汗青"是＿＿＿的詩句。

　　A.文天祥　　　B.岳飛

朗讀

《相見歡》

《過零丁洋》

Lesson Nine

Two Classical Poems

To the Tonal Pattern of *Xiangjianhuan*
[Southern Tang] Li Yu

Wordless I go up the western tower alone
The hooklike moon hanging,
Solitary wutong trees locked up in the deep courtyard
In this chilly and clear autumn standing.
No way to straighten it up,
Worse still if you try.
Grievous it is to part.
Unspeakable feelings in my heart lie.

Crossing the Lonesome Sea
[Southern Song] Wen Tianxiang

Studying hard the classics to protect motherland from childhood,
For four years I fought the invaders with might and main.
The war-torn country looks like willow catkin scattered,
Up and down my life equals to duckweed in wind and rain.
On Terrifying Beach I mentioned how I was terrified,
Crossing Lonesome Sea I felt lonesome and sighed.
It's true from the beginning all men must perish,
It's my loyalty in history I should like to establish.

第十課

現代詩二首

黃河頌

光未然

我站在高山之巔，
望黃河滾滾，
奔向東南。
金濤澎湃，
掀起萬丈狂瀾；
濁流宛轉，
結成九曲連環；

從崑崙山下奔向黃海之邊；

把中原大地劈(pī)成南北兩面。

啊！黃河！

你是中華民族的搖籃！

五千年的古國文化，

從你這兒發源；

多少英雄的故事，

在你身邊扮演！

啊！黃河！

你是偉大堅強，

像一個巨人出現在亞洲平原之上，

用你那英雄的體魄築成我們民族的屏障。

啊！黃河！

你一瀉萬丈，

浩浩蕩蕩，

向南北兩岸伸出千萬條鐵的臂膀。

我們民族的偉大精神，

將要在你的哺育下發揚滋長！

第十課

我們祖國的英雄兒女，

將要學習你的榜樣，

像你一樣的偉大堅強！

像你一樣的偉大堅強！

【注釋】

中原：指黃河中下游地區。

作品簡介

　　《黃河大合唱》創作於抗日戰爭時期（1939年3月），由年輕的詩人光未然作詞，冼(xiǎn)星海作曲。《黃河頌》是《黃河大合唱》中的一個樂章，也是中華民族的頌歌。它以中華民族的發源地之一——黃河為背景，歌頌了中華民族的古老、偉大和堅強，以及中華兒女對這片土地的深愛和永不屈服的精神。《黃河大合唱》氣吞山河，具有鮮明的民族風格，是中國著名的交響音樂。

鄉　愁

余光中

小時候

鄉愁是一枚小小的郵票

我在這頭

母親在那頭

長大後

鄉愁是一張窄窄的船票

我在這頭

新娘在那頭

後來呵

鄉愁是一方矮矮的墳墓

我在外頭

母親呵在裏頭

而現在

鄉愁是一灣淺淺的海峽

我在這頭

大陸在那頭

作品簡介

　　《鄉愁》是台灣著名詩人余光中先生於1971年所寫。詩歌抒發了他內心難以排解的思念故鄉和親人的感情。詩雖不長，卻句句動人。

生詞

sòng 頌	eulogy; ode		hào dàng 浩盪	vast and mighty
shāndiān 山巔	the summit of a mountain		bì bǎng 臂膀	arm and shoulder
péng pài 澎湃	surge describing waves		bǔ yù 哺育	feed; nurture
xiān 掀	stir up; surge		zī zhǎng 滋長	grow
kuáng lán 狂瀾	raging waves		bǎngyàng 榜樣	model; example
wǎnzhuǎn 宛轉	winding		méi 枚	a measure word (for postage stamp, etc.)
wān(彎) qū 曲	curved; bend		yóu piào 郵票	postage stamp
yáo lán 搖籃	cradle			
bàn yǎn 扮演	play the part of		xīn niáng 新娘	bride
tǐ pò 體魄	physique; physical health		fén mù 墳墓	grave; tomb
píngzhàng 屏障	protective screen			

聽寫

頌　掀　扮演　體魄　浩盪　臂膀　榜樣　彎曲　郵票

*哺育　滋長　屏障

比一比

膀 { 臂膀 / 翅膀 }　　滋 { 滋長 / 滋味 }　　扮 { 扮演 / 打扮 }

詞語運用

打扮　扮演

春節晚會上，同學們都打扮得很漂亮。

在這個戲中，哥哥扮演一個壞人的角色。

體魄

我們不但要學習好，而且要有強健的體魄。

跳傘運動員不但要有強健的體魄，而且頭腦要清醒。

多音字

pī
劈
pī
劈開

pǐ
劈
pǐ
劈柴

qū
曲
qū
彎曲

qǔ
曲
qǔ
歌曲

回答問題

1. 閱讀《黃河頌》最後七行，請想一想：詩人用黃河比喻了什麼？（提示：A.不屈的民族精神　B.英雄的體魄）

2. 《鄉愁》表達了詩人什麼樣的感情？（提示：A.思念郵票的感情　B.思念母親的感情　C.思念故鄉和親人的感情）

詞語解釋

鄉愁——思鄉之愁。

海峽——這裏指台灣海峽。

朗誦

《黃河頌》和《鄉愁》

 *English Translation*

Lesson Ten

Two Contemporary Poems

Ode to the Yellow River
Guang Weiran

Standing on the peak of the mountain,
I watch the Yellow River
Rolling south-eastward forever.
In some parts raging torrents rise to the sky,
Mountainous billows and terrible waves swell high.
In some parts muddy currents wind,
Bends, interlinks and zigzag chains we find.
It runs from the foot of Kunlun Mountians
To the front of the Yellow Sea,
Cutting the Central Plains
Into halves - north and south as we see.
O, the Yellow River,
The cradle of the Chinese people!
Five-thousand years' civilization of this ancient nation
Takes root from your principle.
Countless heroic deeds
Happen by your body gracious.
O, the Yellow River,
Great , firm and tenacious
You're like a giant arising
On the plain of Asia.
With your mighty body
You build up the defense for China.
O, the Yellow River!
With unyielding vigor,
In formidable strength rushing
Toward south and north banks
Thousands of iron arms stretching.

Our lofty national spirit and essence,
Under your nurture
Is for ever in development and advance!
The courageous people of our motherland
Will follow your example and stand
As strong and firm as you!
As strong and firm as you!

Homesickness
Yu Guangzhong

When I was at my wee age,
My homesickness was that tiny stamp for postage.
I was at this end
Mother was at the other end.

When I became an adult
My homesickness was that strip of boat ticket.
I was at this end
My bride was at the other end.

With the passing of time
My homesickness was that square low shrine.
I was at its outside
But mother was inside.

Nowadays
My homesickness is that shallow strait.
I am on this side
The mainland is on the other side.

生字表（繁）

1. 篇(piān) 泛(fàn) 映(yìng) 彼(bǐ) 艾(ài) 基(jī) 礎(chǔ) 騷(sāo) 抒(shū) 逐(zhú) 憤(fèn) 掩(yǎn) 涕(tì) 禁(jīn) 索(suǒ)
   遭(zāo) 衰(shuāi) 粽(zòng)

2. 敍(xù) 焦(jiāo) 芝(zhī) 純(chún) 徘(pái) 徊(huái) 侶(lǚ) 勤(qín) 朗(lǎng) 誦(sòng) 嫁(jià) 吏(lì) 嫌(xián) 迫(pò) 嚀(níng)
   吊(diào) 魂(hún) 柏(bǎi) 覆(fù) 葬(zàng) 吟(yín) 郊(jiāo) 慈(cí) 暉(huī)

3. 韻(yùn) 律(lǜ) 登(dēng) 樓(lóu) 廬(lú) 瀑(pù) 烽(fēng) 搔(sāo)

4. 莫(mò) 烹(pēng) 傾(qīng) 聖(shèng) 賢(xián) 寂(jì) 寞(mò) 昔(xī) 宴(yàn) 徑(jìng) 沽(gū) 酌(zhuó) 裘(qiú) 愁(chóu)

5. 伐(fá) 薪(xīn) 鬢(bìn) 憂(yōu) 賤(jiàn) 駕(jià) 輾(niǎn) 飢(jī) 歇(xiē) 翩(piān) 叱(chì) 牽(qiān) 驅(qū) 紗(shā) 綾(líng)
   繫(jì) 值(zhí)

6. 奴(nú) 淘(táo) 豪(háo) 傑(jié) 瑾(jǐn) 姿(zī) 綸(guān) 虜(lǔ)

7. 釵(chāi) 酥(sū) 緒(xù) 盟(méng) 錦(jǐn) 託(tuō) 痕(hén) 殘(cán) 箋(jiān) 斜(xié) 闌(lán) 嚥(yàn)

8. 憑(píng) 瀟(xiāo) 嘯(xiào) 烈(liè) 恥(chǐ) 猶(yóu) 踏(tà) 匈(xiōng) 闕(què)

9. 鈎(gōu) 梧(wú) 桐(tóng) 鎖(suǒ) 剪(jiǎn) 番(fān) 滋(zī) 零(líng) 戈(gē) 寥(liáo) 萍(píng)

10. 頌(sòng) 巔(diān) 澎(péng) 湃(pài) 掀(xiān) 瀾(lán) 宛(wǎn) 曲(qū) 魄(pò) 屏(píng) 障(zhàng) 浩(hào) 臂(bì) 哺(bǔ) 榜(bǎng) 枚(méi) 郵(yóu) 票(piào) 墳(fén)

共計140個生字

生字表（简）

1. piān fàn yìng bǐ ài jī chǔ sāo shū zhú fèn yǎn tì jīn suǒ
   篇 泛 映 彼 艾 基 础 骚 抒 逐 愤 掩 涕 禁 索
   zāo shuāi zòng
   遭 衰 粽

2. xù jiāo zhī chún pái huái lǚ qín lǎng sòng jià lì xián pò níng
   叙 焦 芝 纯 徘 徊 侣 勤 朗 诵 嫁 吏 嫌 迫 咛
   diào hún bǎi fù zàng yín jiāo cí huī
   吊 魂 柏 覆 葬 吟 郊 慈 晖

3. yùn lǜ dēng lóu lú pù fēng sāo
   韵 律 登 楼 庐 瀑 烽 搔

4. mò pēng qīng shèng xián jì mò xī yàn jìng gū zhuó qiú chóu
   莫 烹 倾 圣 贤 寂 寞 昔 宴 径 沽 酌 裘 愁

5. fá xīn bìn yōu jiàn jià niǎn jī xiē piān chì qiān qū shā líng
   伐 薪 鬓 忧 贱 驾 辗 饥 歇 翩 叱 牵 驱 纱 绫
   jì zhí
   系 值

6. nú táo háo jié jǐn zī guān lǔ
   奴 淘 豪 杰 瑾 姿 纶 虏

7. chāi sū xù méng jǐn tuō hén cán jiān xié lán yàn
   钗 酥 绪 盟 锦 托 痕 残 笺 斜 阑 咽

8. píng xiāo xiào liè chǐ yóu tà xiōng què
   凭 潇 啸 烈 耻 犹 踏 匈 阙

9. 钩(gōu) 梧(wú) 桐(tóng) 锁(suǒ) 剪(jiǎn) 番(fān) 滋(zī) 零(líng) 戈(gē) 寥(liáo) 萍(píng)

10. 颂(sòng) 巅(diān) 澎(péng) 湃(pài) 掀(xiān) 澜(lán) 宛(wǎn) 曲(qū) 魄(pò) 屏(píng) 障(zhàng) 浩(hào) 臂(bì) 哺(bǔ) 榜(bǎng) 枚(méi) 邮(yóu) 票(piào) 坟(fén)

生詞表（繁）

1. 收集 篇 廣泛 反映 影響 彼艾 形式 浪漫 基礎
   shōu jí piān guǎngfàn fǎnyìng yǐngxiǎng bǐ ài xíngshì làngmàn jī chǔ

   離騷 抒情 放逐 悲憤 掩涕 禁不住 求索 追求 理想
   lí sāo shūqíng fàngzhú bēi fèn yǎn tì jīn bu zhù qiú suǒ zhuī qiú lǐ xiǎng

   遭遇 貴族 命運 衰落 紀念 粽子
   zāo yù guì zú mìngyùn shuāi luò jì niàn zòng zi

2. 敘事 劉蘭芝 純真 悲劇 徘徊 伴侶 勤勞 （朗）誦 嫁
   xù shì liú lán zhī chúnzhēn bēi jù pái huái bàn lǚ qín láo lǎng sòng jià

   府吏 為難 嫌 逼迫 叮嚀 上吊 魂 松柏 覆蓋
   fǔ lì wéinán xián bī pò dīngníng shàngdiào hún sōngbǎi fù gài

   埋葬 吟 孟郊 慈母 縫（衣） 春暉
   máizàng yín mèngjiāo cí mǔ féng yī chūn huī

3. 固定 音韻 格律 嚴格 工整 動聽 登樓 一層
   gù dìng yīn yùn gé lǜ yán gé gōngzhěng dòngtīng dēng lóu yì céng

   開闊 廬山 瀑布 烽火 搔
   kāi kuò lú shān pù bù fēnghuǒ sāo

4. 莫 烹 傾聽 聖賢 寂寞 昔時 宴 徑（直） 沽 酌
   mò pēng qīngtīng shèngxián jì mò xī shí yàn jìng zhí gū zhuó

   裘 愁
   qiú chóu

5. 伐薪 兩鬢 憂 賤 駕車 輾 飢 歇 翩翩 叱 牽 驅
   fá xīn liǎngbìn yōu jiàn jià chē niǎn jī xiē piānpiān chì qiān qū

   紗 綾 繫 （價）值
   shā líng jì jià zhí

中國詩歌欣賞

6. 念奴嬌(niàn nú jiāo) 淘(táo) 豪傑(háo jié) 公瑾(gōng jǐn) 姿(zī) 綸巾(guān jīn) 強虜(qiáng lǔ)

7. 釵頭鳳(chāi tóu fèng) 酥(sū) (情)緒(qíng xù) 山盟(海誓)(shān méng hǎi shì) 錦託(jǐn tuō) 淚痕(lèi hén) 殘箋(cán jiān) 斜闌(xié lán) 嚥(yàn)

8. 憑(píng) 瀟瀟(xiāoxiāo) 嘯(xiào) 激烈(jī liè) 恥(chǐ) 猶(yóu) 踏(tà) 匈奴(xiōng nú) 闕(què)

9. 鈎(gōu) 梧桐(wú tóng) 鎖(suǒ) 剪(jiǎn) 一番(yì fān) 滋味(zī wèi) 零(líng) 干戈(gān gē) 寥落(liáo luò) (浮)萍(fú píng)

10. 頌(sòng) 山巔(shān diān) 澎湃(péng pài) 掀(xiān) 狂瀾(kuáng lán) 宛轉(wǎn zhuǎn) (彎)曲(wān qū) 搖籃(yáo lán) 扮演(bàn yǎn) 體魄(tǐ pò) 屏障(píng zhàng) 浩蕩(hào dàng) 臂膀(bì bǎng) 哺育(bǔ yù) 滋長(zī zhǎng) 榜樣(bǎng yàng) 一枚(yì méi) 郵票(yóu piào) 新娘(xīn niáng) 墳墓(fén mù)

共計149個生詞

生词表（简）

1. 收集 篇 广泛 反映 影响 彼 艾 形式 浪漫 基础
   离骚 抒情 放逐 悲愤 掩涕 禁不住 求索 追求 理想
   遭遇 贵族 命运 衰落 纪念 粽子

2. 叙事 刘兰芝 纯真 悲剧 徘徊 伴侣 勤劳 （朗）诵 嫁
   府吏 为难 嫌 逼迫 叮咛 上吊 魂 松柏 覆盖
   埋葬 吟 孟郊 慈母 缝（衣） 春晖

3. 固定 音韵 格律 严格 工整 动听 登 楼 一层
   开阔 庐山 瀑布 烽火 搔

4. 莫 烹 倾听 圣贤 寂寞 昔时 宴 径（直） 沽 酌
   裘 愁

5. 伐薪 两鬓 忧 贱 驾车 辗 饥 歇 翩翩 叱 牵 驱
   纱 绫 系 （价）值

中國詩歌欣賞

6. 念奴娇 淘 豪杰 公瑾 姿 纶巾 强虏

7. 钗头凤 酥 （情）绪 山盟（海誓） 锦 托 泪痕 残笺

斜 阑 咽

8. 凭 潇潇 啸 激烈 耻 犹 踏 匈奴 阙

9. 钩 梧桐 锁 剪 一番 滋味 零 干戈 寥落 （浮）萍

10. 颂 山巅 澎湃 掀 狂澜 宛转 （弯）曲 摇篮 扮演

体魄 屏障 浩荡 臂膀 哺育 滋长 榜样 一枚

邮票 新娘 坟墓

共计149个生词

第二課

一　寫生詞

敍	事											
焦												
劉	蘭	芝										
純	真											
徘	徊											
伴	侶											
勤	勞											
朗	誦											
嫁												
府	吏											
嫌												
逼	迫											

叮嚀											
上吊											
魂											
松柏											
覆蓋											
埋葬											
吟											
孟郊											
慈母											
暉											

二 組詞

徘_____　誦_____　勤_____　迫_____

慈_____　侶_____　純_____　郊_____

葬_____　覆_____　柏_____　敘_____

三 選字組詞

（朗　郎）誦　　　官（史　吏）　　　（歡　嫌）棄

女（朗　郎）　　　歷（史　吏）　　　道（歡　嫌）

四 抄寫詩歌《遊子吟》一遍，並翻譯成白話

遊子吟

_____　　　_____

_____　　　_____

_____　　　_____

譯文：

_____

_____

_____

_____

_____

_____

五 將《孔雀東南飛》下列兩段詩句翻譯成白話

十七為君婦

心中常苦悲

雞鳴入機織

夜夜不得息

三日斷五匹

大人故嫌遲

六　根據課文選擇正確答案

1. 樂府開始於_____。

　　A 漢代　　　　B 戰國　　　　C 春秋

2. 《孔雀東南飛》是_____。

　　A 漢樂府詩　　B 楚辭　　　　C 詩經

3. 《遊子吟》的作者是_____。

　　A 屈原　　　　B 孟郊

七　詞語解釋

1. 臨行——

2. 暉——

3. 遲——

4. 心急如火——

八　背誦《遊子吟》

第四課

一 寫生詞

莫												
烹												
傾	聽											
聖	賢											
寂	寞											
昔	時											
宴												
徑	直											
沽												
酌												
裘												
愁												

二 組詞

宴_____ 聖_____ 傾_____ 烹_____

昔_____ 愁_____ 寂_____ 賢_____

三 抄寫詩歌《將進酒》前八句

四 填空組詞

　　　　　　會　　　　聽　　　　賢

宴_____　　聖_____　　傾_____

五 根據課文選擇正確答案

1. 《將進酒》的作者是_____。

    A 杜甫　　　B 李白　　　C 白居易

2. "君不見高堂明鏡悲白髮,朝如青絲暮成雪"意思是_____。

    A 在鏡子中看到自己頭髮白了

    B 感到時間過得飛快,人生短暫

3. "天生我材必有用,千金散盡還復來"意思是_____。

    A 自信有能力成就大事業,並不在乎金錢

    B 花錢大方

六　詞語解釋

　　1. 君——

　　2. 昔時——

　　3. 聖賢——

　　4. 烹——

　　5. 裘——

七　把詩歌《將進酒》中你喜歡的句子寫下來

_____

_____

_____

_____

_____

_____

_____

八　背誦並默寫《將進酒》前八句

第六課

一 寫生詞

奴												
淘												
豪	傑											
公	瑾											
姿												
綸	巾											
虜												

二 組詞

壁_____ 淘_____ 豪_____ 傑_____

姿_____ 虜_____ 濤_____ 奴_____

三 選字組詞

　　雄(次　姿)　　　(毫　豪)傑　　　回(家　嫁)

　　一(次　姿)　　　(毫　豪)毛　　　(家　嫁)女兒

四 抄寫《念奴嬌‧赤壁懷古》一遍(左邊寫上闋（què）)

　　　　念奴嬌‧赤壁懷古

五 根據課文選擇正確答案

1. 《念奴嬌·赤壁懷古》的作者是_____。

   A 杜甫　　　B 李白　　　C 蘇軾

2. 《念奴嬌·赤壁懷古》是_____。

   A 唐詩　　　B 宋詞　　　C 楚辭

3. 蘇軾是_____的大文學家。

   A 戰國時期　B 宋朝　　　C 唐朝

六 詞語解釋

1. 懷古——
2. 風流人物——
3. 強虜——
4. 豪傑——

七 把《念奴嬌·赤壁懷古》中你喜歡的句子再寫一遍

_____

_____

_____

八 背誦《念奴嬌·赤壁懷古》

九 默寫《念奴嬌·赤壁懷古》中你喜歡的句子(不少於四句)

第八課

一 寫生詞

憑											
瀟	瀟										
嘯											
激	烈										
恥											
猶											
踏											
匈	奴										
闕											

二 抄寫《滿江紅・寫懷》一遍（左邊寫上闋 que）

滿江紅・寫懷

_____   _____

_____   _____

_____   _____

_____   _____

_____   _____

_____   _____

_____   _____

_____   _____

_____   _____

_____   _____

三 根據課文選擇正確答案

   1.《滿江紅・寫懷》的作者是_____。

     A 岳飛　　　B 蘇軾　　　C 李白

2. 岳飛是＿＿＿＿＿＿人。

　　A 漢朝　　　　B 唐朝　　　　C 宋朝

3. "莫等閑、白了少年頭，空悲切"的意思是＿＿＿＿＿＿。

　　A 年齡很小頭髮就白了，很悲傷

　　B 不要叫時光輕易流走，結果一事無成而悲傷

4. 《滿江紅‧寫懷》表達了岳飛＿＿＿＿＿＿。

　　A 希望報仇雪恨、收回國土的悲壯心情

　　B 收復國土的快樂心情

四　詞語解釋

1. 怒髮衝冠——

2. 瀟瀟——

3. 壯懷激烈——

4. 胡虜——

五　背誦《滿江紅‧寫懷》

六　默寫《滿江紅‧寫懷》第一段

第十課

一　寫生詞

頌											
山	巔										
澎	湃										
掀											
狂	瀾										
宛	轉										
彎	曲										
體	魄										
屏	障										
浩	蕩										
臂	膀										
哺	育										

榜	樣									
一	枚									
郵	票									
墳	墓									

二　組詞

頌＿＿＿　　澎＿＿＿　　掀＿＿＿　　狂＿＿＿

扮＿＿＿　　曲＿＿＿　　榜＿＿＿　　魄＿＿＿

屏＿＿＿　　浩＿＿＿　　臂＿＿＿　　墳＿＿＿

票＿＿＿　　郵＿＿＿　　搖＿＿＿　　堅＿＿＿

三　選字組詞

（浩　告）盪　　（旁　榜）邊　　（分　扮）演

（浩　告）訴　　（旁　榜）樣　　（分　扮）開

（漂　票）亮　　（郵　睡）寄　　（墳　憤）墓

郵（漂　票）　　（郵　睡）覺　　悲（墳　憤）

四 抄寫《黃河頌》選段和《鄉愁》全詩一遍（左起從上向下寫）

啊！黃河！

你是中華民族的搖籃！

五千年的古國文化，

從你這兒發源；

多少英雄的故事，

在你身邊扮演！

鄉愁

五 根據課文選擇正確答案

　　1.《黃河頌》的作者是_____。

　　　A 光未然　　　　　B 余光中

　　2.《黃河頌》歌頌了_____。

　　　A 黃河的壯觀和古老

　　　B 中華民族永不屈服的精神

　　3.《黃河大合唱》寫於_____。

　　　A 宋朝　　　　　　B 抗日戰爭時期

　　4.《鄉愁》的作者是_____。

　　　A 光未然　　　　　B 余光中

　　5.《鄉愁》抒發了作者_____的感情。

　　　A 思念母親　　　　B 思念故鄉和親人

六 朗誦《黃河頌》、《鄉愁》各三遍

第二課聽寫

第四課聽寫

第六課聽寫

第八課聽寫

第十課聽寫

中國詩歌欣賞

第一課

一　寫生詞

篇												
廣泛												
反映												
彼												
艾												
基礎												
離騷												
抒情												
放逐												
悲憤												
掩												
涕												
禁不住												

求	索										
遭	遇										
衰	落										
粽	子										

二 組詞

基＿＿＿＿　　抒＿＿＿＿　　遭＿＿＿＿　　逐＿＿＿＿

憤＿＿＿＿　　掩＿＿＿＿　　篇＿＿＿＿　　索＿＿＿＿

粽＿＿＿＿　　衰＿＿＿＿　　泛＿＿＿＿　　禁＿＿＿＿

三 選字組詞

（構　溝）成　　　　　　浪（慢　漫）

河（構　溝）　　　　　　快（慢　漫）

四 抄寫詩歌《採葛》一遍

_____

_____

_____

五 抄寫詩句"路漫漫其修遠兮,吾將上下而求索"
兮
xī

兩遍

_____

_____

六 根據課文選擇正確答案

1.《詩經》是中國第一部_____。

　A 歷史書　　　　B 詩歌總集　　　C 小說

2.《詩經》大約成書於_____。

　A 公元6世紀　　B 公元600年　　C 公元前6世紀

3.《採葛》選自_____。

　A《詩經》　　　B《楚辭》

4. 屈原是_____楚國人。

　A 春秋時期　　　B 戰國時期

5. 屈原是中國第一位偉大的詩人。他創造了新的詩歌形式_____。

　A 楚辭　　　　　B 詩經

6. 屈原的作品中最著名的是_____。

　　A《詩經》　　　　B《離騷》

7. 中國詩歌的源頭是由_____共同構成的。

　　A《離騷》　　　　B《詩經》　　　　C 楚辭與《詩經》

8. 端午節是為了紀念屈原，主要活動有_____。

　　A 舞獅　　　　　B 吃餃子　　　　　C 賽龍船、吃粽子

七　背誦並默寫

1. 《採葛》。

2. 詩句"路漫漫其修遠兮，吾將上下而求索"。

第三課

一　寫生詞

音	韻										
格	律										
登											
樓											
廬	山										
瀑	布										
烽	火										
搔											

二　組詞

音_____　　格_____　　登_____　　樓_____

三 抄寫下列詩歌一遍

登<ruby>鸛<rt>guàn</rt></ruby>雀樓

_____

_____

_____

_____

望廬山瀑布

_____

_____

_____

_____

春望

_____

_____

_____

_____

四 任選《登鸛雀樓》或《望廬山瀑布》中一首翻譯成白話

_____

_____

_____

_____

_____

五 選詞填空

李白　　王之渙(huàn)　　杜甫(fǔ)　　白居易

五言律詩　　七言絕句　　五言絕句

1.《登鸛雀樓》的作者是＿＿＿＿＿＿。

2.《望廬山瀑布》的作者是＿＿＿＿＿＿。

3.《春望》的作者是＿＿＿＿＿＿。

4.《登鸛雀樓》是一首＿＿＿＿＿＿。

5.《望廬山瀑布》是一首＿＿＿＿＿＿。

6.《春望》是一首＿＿＿＿＿＿。

7. 唐代最著名的詩人有＿＿＿＿＿、＿＿＿＿＿和＿＿＿＿＿等。

六 詞語解釋

1. 依——

2. 欲——

3. 盡——

4. 窮——

5. 短——

6. 渾——

七 連線

    五言絕句   全詩四句，每句七字

    七言絕句   全詩八句，每句五字

    五言律詩   全詩四句，每句五字

    七言律詩   全詩八句，每句七字

八 背誦並默寫《登鸛雀樓》和《望廬山瀑布》兩首詩（"鸛"字可以寫拼音）

第五課

一 寫生詞

伐	薪											
兩	鬢											
憂												
賤												
駕	車											
輾												
飢												
歇												
翩	翩											
叱												
牽												

驅										
紗										
綾										
繫										
價	值									

二　組詞

伐_____　　繫_____　　憂_____　　駕_____

鬢_____　　牽_____　　歇_____　　飢_____

賤_____

三　選字組詞

伐（薪　新）　　（飢　肌）餓　　（代　伐）木

（薪　新）書　　（飢　肌）肉　　古（伐　代）

（紗　沙）布　　貴（賤　淺）　　價（植　值）

（紗　沙）土　　深（賤　淺）　　（植　值）物

四 抄寫《賣炭翁》前八行

　

五 反義詞填空

　　　　　　　飽　放心　貴

賤——（　　）　飢——（　　）　擔憂——（　　　）

六 選擇填空

1. 多吃有＿＿＿＿＿＿＿的食物有利於身體健康。

（營養　經營）

2. 這個書店＿＿＿＿＿＿＿得很好，來買書的人越來越多。

（營養　經營）

3. 妹妹把新衣服弄髒了，真_____。（可惜　愛惜）

4. 小華十分_____她的書。（可惜　愛惜）

5. 賣炭翁的作者是_____。（李白　杜甫(fǔ)　白居易）

七　根據課文判斷對錯

1. 賣炭翁賣炭的錢準備用來蓋房子。　　___對　___錯

2. 賣炭翁穿的衣服很少。　　___對　___錯

3. 為了炭能賣得貴一些，賣炭翁希望天氣寒冷。　　___對　___錯

4. 賣炭翁進城一會兒就把炭賣完了。　　___對　___錯

5. 來了兩個騎馬的老百姓要買炭。　　___對　___錯

6. 一車炭重量不到一千斤。　　___對　___錯

7. 半匹紅紗、一丈綾與一車炭的價值一樣。　___對　___錯

八 造句

  1. 擔憂＿＿＿＿＿＿＿＿＿＿＿＿＿＿＿＿＿＿＿＿

  2. 價值＿＿＿＿＿＿＿＿＿＿＿＿＿＿＿＿＿＿＿＿

  3. 飢餓＿＿＿＿＿＿＿＿＿＿＿＿＿＿＿＿＿＿＿＿

九 背誦並默寫《賣炭翁》前八句

第七課

一 寫生詞

釵												
酥												
情	緒											
山	盟											
錦												
託												
淚	痕											
殘												
箋												
斜												
闌												
嚥												

二 組詞

　　　釵_____　　盟_____　　緒_____　　痕_____

　　　錦_____　　託_____　　斜_____　　嚥_____

三 抄寫陸游的《釵頭鳳》一遍（左邊寫上闋^{què}）

　　　　　　　釵頭鳳　（陸游）

_____　　_____
_____　　_____
_____　　_____
_____　　_____
_____　　_____

四 抄寫唐琬^{wǎn}的《釵頭鳳》一遍（左邊寫上闋^{què}）

　　　　　　　釵頭鳳　（唐琬）

_____　　_____
_____　　_____

_____   _____

_____   _____

_____   _____

五 根據課文選擇正確答案

1. 陸游是_____人。

   A 漢朝　　　B 唐朝　　　C 南宋

2. 陸游的《釵頭鳳》是一首_____。

   A 詩　　　　B 詞　　　　C 楚辭

六 詞語解釋

1. 一懷愁緒——

2. 淚痕殘——

3. 離索——

4. 曉風——

七　背誦《釵頭鳳》(陸游)

八　默寫《釵頭鳳》(陸游)第一段(生字可以寫拼音)

第九課

一　寫生詞

鈎											
梧桐											
鎖											
剪											
一番											
滋味											
零											
干戈											
寥落											
浮萍											

二　組詞

鈎_____　　鎖_____　　剪_____　　滋_____

戈_____　　番_____　　萍_____　　梧_____

三 抄寫《相見歡》和《過零丁洋》

相見歡

過零丁洋

_____

_____

四 根據課文選擇正確答案

1. 《相見歡》(無言獨上西樓)的作者是_____。

   A 李白　　　　　　　　B 李煜(yù)

2. 李煜是南唐的_____。

   A 皇帝　　　　　　　　B 將軍

3. "人生自古誰無死,留取丹心照汗青"是_____的詩句。

   A 文天祥(xiáng)　　　　B 岳飛

五 詞語解釋

1. 逢——

2. 身世——

3. 四周星——

4. 汗青——

六　把《相見歡》和《過零丁洋》中你喜歡的句子寫下來
　　（每首選四句，左右分別寫）

　　_____　　　_____

　　_____　　　_____

　　_____　　　_____

　　_____　　　_____

七　背誦《相見歡》和《過零丁洋》

八　默寫《相見歡》后四句和《過零丁洋》最后兩句

第一課聽寫

第三課聽寫

第五課聽寫

第七課聽寫

第九課聽寫

中國詩歌欣賞